# CHEETAHS

First published in Great Britain in 2000 by
Colin Baxter Photography Ltd
Grantown-on-Spey
PH26 3NA
Scotland
www.worldlifelibrary.co.uk

Text © Luke Hunter 2000
Photographs © Luke Hunter 2000
Map © Wendy Price Cartographic Services 2000
Map redrawn from Nowell, K. & Jackson, P. 1996. Wild Cats: Status Survey and
Conservation Action Plan, IUCN, Gland, Switzerland.

WorldLife Library Series

A CIP Catalogue record for this book is available from the British Library.

ISBN 1-900455-64-1

Printed in China

# CHEETAHS

Colin Baxter Photography, Grantown-on-Spey, Scotland

# Contents

Evolution, Form and Function     7

Predator and Prey     17

The Sometimes Social Cat     29

The Next Generation     39

The Imperiled Speedster     53

Racing Against Extinction     63

Distribution Map     68

Cheetah Facts     69

Recommended Reading     70

Useful Contacts / Biographical Note     71

Index     72

# Evolution, Form and Function

Somewhere on the grasslands of Africa, as you read these words, a mother cheetah is hunting. She is in no apparent hurry but her senses are primed as she systematically quarters the high grass. Her three cubs are playing endless games of chase around her, oblivious to the mother's efforts to locate their next meal. Cubs often spoil hunts by alerting potential prey but on this occasion, the youngsters' frantic play flushes a steenbok, a small antelope which crouches motionless in long grass, hoping predators will simply walk on by. The mother cheetah had done precisely that, but just as her lagging cubs disturb the little antelope, she glances behind her. In a second, her relaxed, sinuous walk transforms into a blur of spotted fur and dust. The steenbok has a good start but it is no match for the fastest mammal on earth. Repeatedly, just when it appears the cheetah is running as fast as she possibly could, she switches gear and accelerates even further. At speeds almost too fast to follow, she narrows the prey's lead with ground-eating strides. Despite the steenbok's frantic last-minute efforts to dodge her, the mother cheetah bowls it over with a deft flick, and both of them disappear in the long grass. Ten seconds after the chase has begun, there is nothing to see except for a 1000-foot-long (300-meter-long) curtain of dust hanging in the air.

Quite unlike any other predator on earth, the cheetah ('cita' is Hindi for 'spotted one') is one of the most specialized carnivores in the world. Unsurpassed as a sprinter, it combines the explosive power of the cat family with the pursuit tactics of dogs to exploit a predatory niche it alone occupies. Yet, despite its unique specialization, we know relatively little about the cheetah's ancestry. The earliest record of the modern cheetah, *Acinonyx jubatus*, is from southern and east Africa around three-and-a-half million years ago. Its ancestors probably split from other large cats (lions, tigers, leopards and jaguars which belong in a separate genus, *Panthera*) around five million years ago, in a distinct lineage which ultimately produced today's cheetahs, pumas and

*Cheetah country; long grass provides safe refuges for cubs and cover for adults on the hunt.*

a small South American cat called the jaguarundi.

Unfortunately, paleontologists have yet to discover fossil evidence of its immediate precursors, but we do know a good deal about some of its relatives existing around the same time. Up until 500,000 years ago, a giant cheetah *Acinonyx pardinensis* hunted on the open steppes of Europe, China and India. About the same size as a modern lioness, it had the same, super-sprinting build of the modern cheetah but weighed almost twice as much – around 209-220 lb (95-100 kg), compared with the 110-132 lb (50-60 kg) of today's cheetahs. Given its larger build, it could not quite have reached the speeds attained by the modern cheetah but nonetheless, *Acinonyx pardinensis* at full stretch on the European plains must have been an extraordinary sight. Cheetah-like cats also arose in North America around the same time and one species survived as recently as 10,000 years ago. Their exact relationship to modern cheetahs is still disputed, but they show very similar body specializations to cheetahs and seem to share a common ancestor. They also have anatomical similarities to modern pumas, hence the theory that cheetahs and pumas sit closely on the feline family tree, a hypothesis recently corroborated by modern molecular analysis.

Regardless of its ancestry, the modern cheetah is the last surviving sprinting cat. Taxonomists, the specialized biologists who classify organisms, divide cheetahs into five sub-species or races. These divisions are based largely on geography rather than any demonstrated difference between populations and may not be well founded. For example, cheetahs from east Africa and cheetahs from southern Africa are considered two separate sub-species; however, the genetic distance between these two populations is up to 100 times less than the differences between human racial groups. In other words, genetically speaking, there is no significant difference between cheetahs from the two regions. It's likely that, with more research, the number of sub-species will be reduced.

About 75 years ago, zoologists believed they had discovered an entirely new cheetah species. In 1926, a cheetah with beautifully rich black stripes and mottled markings was shot in Rhodesia (now called Zimbabwe). So different was the cat from the normal cheetah that it was named as a separate species – *Acinonyx rex*, the king

*Even at 6 months old, like these cubs sunning themselves on a termite mound, cheetahs outclass most other sprinters. Cubs this age can outrun danger and are fast enough (though not necessarily experienced enough) to run down hares.*

cheetah. Controversy raged for decades over the true status of the king cheetah, with disparate theories suggesting it was a distinct species, an aberrant variation of the normal cheetah and even that it was a cheetah–leopard hybrid. The arguments were finally put to rest in 1981 when a king cub was born in captivity to normally spotted parents. We now know that the king pattern arises from a recessive mutation to a single gene controlling spot formation, and despite its extraordinary coat, the king is no different to the spotted cheetah and every bit as much *Acinonyx jubatus*. Kings and normally spotted cheetahs can be born in the same litter, although a king pair can only have king cubs. Up until recently, this striking variant was known only from a localized region around northeastern South Africa (including the Kruger National Park), Zimbabwe and eastern Botswana, but in 1988, a king cheetah skin was recovered from a poacher in the west African country of Burkina Faso.

Whether king or spotted, of all the cheetah's unique characteristics, none has been as celebrated as its fabled speed. Naturalists and scientists have speculated for decades on how fast it can run, a figure which still has not been reliably established. We do know that it can reach at least 65 mph (105 kmph) which is faster than any other animal on land. However, that is almost certainly not the upper limit and a cheetah at full sprint in ideal conditions can probably reach 68-71 mph (110-115 kmph), at least for a few seconds during the chase. This is most likely the fastest speed ever attained by any land mammal – living or extinct – and is quite extraordinary when one realizes it is more or less equivalent to the speed limits imposed on motorists on many highways around the world. Possibly even more remarkable is that in the first two seconds of the chase, it will have passed the 47 mph (75 kmph) mark, which is about twice as fast as an Olympic sprinter.

But just how does the cheetah achieve these breathtaking velocities? Evolution has equipped the cheetah with some highly specialized modifications to the basic cat form.

*Termite mounds are convenient vantage points for*
*spotting prey, and for females with cubs, other predators.*

Its lean, dog-like legs, the most elongate of any large cat, enable it to lengthen its stride, which may be as great as 32 ft (10 m). Although they appear frail, the legs are surprisingly robust. The bones of the lower hind leg are bound tightly together with fibrous tissue allowing very little rotation. This is crucial for stability at high speeds, ensuring the cheetah avoids stumbling or incurring injuries from the phenomenal stresses imposed during the chase. I once experienced the explosive power of these legs at close quarters when changing the radio-collar on a semi-sedated cheetah. As I leant over the diminutive adult female, who was still extremely woozy from the drugs, a nervous kick from her hind legs caught me across the chest and left me sprawling in the grass 6 ft (2 m) away.

Like a sprinter who enhances natural speed with high-tech shoes, the cheetah's unique paws are a critical part of the design for speed. They are also the reason early naturalists were confused about the cheetah's affiliations – dog or cat. Indeed, that the cheetah belongs in the dog family (or, at least, is more closely related to them than to cats) is a misconception that still persists today. Indisputably a cat, the cheetah has paws which appear dog-like but the similarity is only skin-deep. Like all cats, they have the intricate arrangement of ligaments in each toe that allows the family to retract their claws: however, in cheetahs, the mechanism is feeble, resulting in reduced movement and giving rise to another myth, that cheetahs' claws are non-retractile. Contributing to this misunderstanding, they lack the protective sheath of skin which houses the claws of other cat species and hides them from sight. The cheetah's protruding claws act like runners' spikes to enhance grip and their blunt dog-like appearance is more a result of wear-and-tear than design. The claws of cubs remain sharp until they are many months old and cheetahs kept in captivity often have claws almost as sharp and cat-like as any feline. Besides the sophisticated refinements of the claws, the pads of the feet are extremely hard and heavily ridged to increase traction as well as being pointed at the

*With their dog-like builds, cheetahs are poor climbers*
*but lower branches make excellent apparatus for playful cubs.*

front, possibly to assist rapid breaking. Even the cheetah's fifth 'limb', the tail, plays a role; being long, tubular and muscular, it provides counter-balance for rapid changes of direction during the chase.

Assisting the highly specialized limbs is an entire suite of further modifications. Among the large cats, cheetahs have proportionally the longest and most flexible spine. By arching and flexing the spine, the terrific stride length delivered by the legs is augmented a further 10-15 per cent. Indeed, seen in slow motion, the spring-like bunching and uncoiling of the spine is the most apparent feature of the cheetah's gallop. Stride length is further enhanced by having a much reduced collar bone (or clavicle), freeing up the shoulder joint which is able to move in a very broad, fluid arc.

Less obvious adaptations for speed can be found in the cheetah's small head. Shortened jaws reduce weight and house smaller canine teeth than in other big cats. The reduced roots of the canines make room for an enlarged nasal cavity, important for increased air intake while the cheetah suffocates its prey. This allows the exhausted cat to maintain the throttling throat hold and still be able to inhale to recover from the sprint. A deep chest cavity houses enlarged lungs and bronchi (air passages) which, combined with the action of the large heart and highly muscular arteries, ensure the maximum delivery of oxygen. Cheetahs are probably pushed to their physiological limit during the chase. Their body temperature may soar to 104°F (40°C) and their breathing rate frequently tops 150 breaths per minute, close to ten times the resting respiratory rate.

Anatomy and adaptation aside, to watch a cheetah at full stretch is to witness nature at its most spectacular and there is nothing quite like seeing a 60 mph (100 kmph) pursuit on the open grasslands of Africa. But, of course, evolution did not equip the world's fastest sprinter merely to astonish human onlookers. The cheetah's speed is its livelihood. And as we will see in the next chapter, making a living as a cheetah requires a good deal more than simply being fast.

*Despite reducing visibility, winter morning mist*
*provides useful cover and cheetahs actively hunt in foggy conditions.*

# Predator and Prey

The cheetah is usually portrayed as an open plains inhabitant, specializing on small-to-medium-sized antelopes like gazelles and impalas. In most cases, this is not far from the truth. Most studies of cheetahs confirm that, where possible, they concentrate on herbivores such as the 44-55 lb (20-25 kg) Thomson's gazelle ranging up to the impala whose top weight is about 143 lb (65 kg).

Cheetahs also tend to prefer young animals, taking far more than they would if they were simply preying on them 'at random'. This is worth dealing with in a little more detail as it is interesting how scientists calculate such figures and one needs to be careful when talking of the 'preferences' of a predator. In essence, it's very simple and requires only two figures: the numbers of available prey (of different species, ages, sexes and so on) and the numbers of prey actually taken. We then compare what was available for the cheetah and what it actually took. For example, Claire FitzGibbon, who studied the cheetahs of the Serengeti plains, calculated that young Thomson's gazelles made up about 6 per cent of the population but they constituted almost 54 per cent of cheetah kills. Assuming the figures are accurate, we can then say with confidence that cheetahs are actually selecting young Thomson's gazelles in preference to adults. It sounds easy, but it requires many thousands of hours of observing cheetahs and counting antelopes to ensure our figures represent what is actually taking place.

*Cheetahs are at their most vigilant when feeding.*

Calculations aside, the patterns we see in the cheetah's hunting behavior make perfect sense. Unlike lions, whose prodigious strength enables even a solitary lioness to overcome an adult zebra weighing over twice as much, cheetahs are not built for wrestling large, dangerous animals to the ground. By selecting small-to-medium-sized antelopes and concentrating on young animals, the cheetah diminishes the risks of injury during the hunt – crucial for an animal that relies on being in absolute peak condition every time it needs to eat.

However, it would be a mistake to think that is the entire story. Cheetahs are proving to be far more adaptable than is generally thought and studies in 'atypical' cheetah habitat are illustrating that they do not always conform to the vision we have of them as gazelle specialists. While the open plains of Tanzania are probably ideal terrain for the high-speed chase, cheetahs exist in many different habitats and they need to be versatile to survive. In South Africa's densely vegetated Zululand region, cheetahs specialize in hunting nyalas, a woodland antelope which, at 265 lb (120 kg) in the male, is many times heavier than any gazelle species.

Even more impressive, I've seen pairs of male cheetahs hunt young giraffes in thick *Acacia* bush where the cheetahs have the advantage. In open country, adult giraffes cluster protectively around the youngsters and cheetahs risk death from a well-aimed kick if they are foolhardy enough to challenge the defense. But in the tangle of thick woodland and by hunting in pairs or trios, it is far easier for the cheetahs to distract the parents and so isolate a youngster.

Young giraffes are rare targets for cheetahs but are by no means the most unusual. Although cats usually shun the meat of other carnivores, cheetahs in the Kalahari desert sometimes kill Cape foxes and bat-eared foxes, and jackals have been recorded as occasional prey in east Africa. Cheetahs ignore small birds but ostriches, Kori bustards and guinea fowl are fair game. Gus van Dyk, working in South Africa's Pilanesberg National Park, has even recorded them killing baboons, though this is extremely rare and very dangerous. Baboon males have canine teeth as long and sharp as a leopard's and, with their formidable strength, make lethal opponents. Cheetahs normally give baboons a wide

*At around 220 lb (100 kg), this young giraffe is a large kill for cheetahs but not the largest. Occasionally, male coalitions tackle prey as large as adult wildebeests weighing up to 440 lb (200 kg).*

The cheetah's characteristic 'tear streaks' are a mystery. Theories abound,
but they probably enhance facial expressions for communicating important moods,
like aggression, and they might also reduce reflected glare when hunting.

berth but, as the Pilanesberg studies show, they very occasionally take youngsters that have become separated from their troop.

Most cat species hunt at night, but cheetahs are primarily diurnal (daytime) hunters, with peaks of activity early in the morning and towards the end of the afternoon. High-speed chases require maximum visibility to avoid obstacles which might twist an ankle or worse. Additionally, their main enemies, lions and spotted hyenas, are largely nocturnal (night-time) hunters; cheetahs reduce the chances of conflict by hunting outside the active periods of these larger, dangerous competitors. Although cheetahs do see quite well at night, they almost never hunt then, and I have watched them pass within 100 ft (30 m) of apparently easy targets and ignore them. There are, however, always exceptions to the 'rules' of animal behavior and very rarely, they have been observed hunting by full moon in Namibia's Etosha National Park, where the terrain is extremely flat and reflection from the bleached calcrete soils enhances visibility. Cheetahs in the open expanses of the Sahara desert are also reputed to hunt by night.

Hunting during the day also makes the best use of the cheetah's sharpest sense, vision. An actively hunting cheetah 'patrols,' walking steadily along while constantly searching for possible targets. Intermittently, they scan the surroundings from high points such as large trees, termite mounds and, in areas where they are very used to tourists, vehicle roofs. Their vision during the day is extremely keen. As far as I know, no-one has made accurate measurements but they easily pick out distant antelopes over 1¼ miles (2 km) away and recognize prey animals which people can barely see with binoculars.

Once prey is spotted, the cheetah has a repertoire of different tactics it might employ. Having sacrificed stamina for their phenomenal speed, cheetahs can only maintain the chase for between 985-1640 ft (300-500 m). Accordingly, it's no use launching a hunt from hundreds of feet away, particularly when one realizes that the quarry may also be extremely fleet-of-foot. It's no coincidence that, second to the cheetah, their primary prey, gazelles, are the next fastest mammals on land, reaching speeds just below 60 mph (100 kmph). Combined with greater staying power, their chances of escape are high unless the cheetah can approach closely enough for its remarkable acceleration to counteract the prey's blend of speed and stamina. Usually this entails a traditional feline stalk, hiding behind available cover such as bushes and remaining immobile for long periods to bring itself to within 200-230 ft (60-70 m) of the herd. Sometimes, if there is no cover or if the target is unaware it has been spotted, a cheetah will approach in full view of the prey, often freezing or dropping to the ground if the prey looks up. Either way, the aim is to be fairly close before unleashing the final, devastating rush. Importantly though, if very young lambs are present, cheetahs make little effort at concealment and

*A careful stalk begins the hunt.*

may begin their run from hundreds of feet away. Young antelopes are fast, but are no match for adult cheetahs, and their hunting success on lambs is 100 per cent.

As we have already seen with the giraffe-hunters of Zululand, when cheetahs live in areas of dense bush, they rely more on the element of confusion than flat-out speed. In intermediate habitats, such as open savanna interspersed with scattered thickets of dense vegetation, they have yet another tactic. They move from one thicket to another, searching for small prey such as hares and small antelopes like duikers and steenboks, which they flush into the open and run down. For young cheetahs which have recently become independent, this method probably ensures their survival. Although the kills are small, they are relatively easy to make and don't require the precision and timing that are crucial for taking down larger species. For young, inexperienced cheetahs, these will come with time and practice.

Whereas most predators would probably prefer prey to stand still, cheetahs actually depend upon their quarry taking flight to make the kill. A successful hunt relies on them

*Three males on the hunt. It's difficult to tell if cheetahs actually coordinate their tactics in any sort of planned strategy when hunting, but group members do fan out like this, possibly increasing their chances of success.*

being able to trip their prey at high speeds. This is particularly important with larger species which could be dangerous for the cheetah to wrestle to the ground. In some instances when prey fails to flee, cheetahs attempt to wrench the animal off its feet using the 'dew claw' – the cheetah's hook-like equivalent of our thumb which, unlike the other claws, doesn't touch the ground and remains sharp. However, the possibility of being injured by a horn or tusk is far greater and they are just as likely to abandon the hunt when faced by belligerent prey not behaving as it's 'supposed' to.

Clearly, there are many factors at work during a hunt and any single element going awry can thwart the cheetah's best effort. Nonetheless, they are successful in approximately 40-50 per cent of attempts, compared with a success rate of around 25 per cent for lions. Like most cats, cheetahs kill by suffocating their prey with a throttling throat bite which delivers death in around five to ten minutes. Very small prey such as hares and young antelopes may be bitten through the skull, killing them instantly. Once a kill has been made, cheetahs usually drag it to cover as quickly as possible. All the larger African predators – lions, hyenas, leopards and wild dogs – can dominate them and cheetahs lose many kills to 'klepto-parasitism' – the theft of their kills. They sometimes relinquish kills even to large gatherings of vultures, probably because of the increased chance that other predators will notice; lions and hyenas often take their cues from vultures and large congregations act as a signpost to a sure meal. Although cheetahs can easily defend their kills from vultures, the chance that lions might suddenly turn up is sometimes enough to force them to leave.

Their vulnerability while eating leads them to bolt their food quickly, while constantly looking around for the approach of other predators. They tend to abandon kills fairly quickly, sometimes leaving considerable amounts of meat. This has led to them being characterized as 'wasteful' and inclined to kill for pleasure, both of which are myths. In areas where other predators are rare, they seldom leave kills before they are completely finished and may spend up to 28 hours feeding on a single carcass. They typically move away from the kill upon nightfall (when other predators are active) but return to it the following morning, behavior which has not been observed where lions and hyenas are common.

So, far from being wasteful, cheetahs essentially kill only when they need to, which is about every one to three days, depending on the size of the prey and the number of cheetahs in a group. On average, an adult needs about 9-11 lb (4-5 kg) of meat per day and can eat a maximum of 22-35 lb (10-16 kg) in a single sitting. A single cheetah could survive if it were to kill one small antelope every day, or alternatively a larger antelope every two or three days. Male cheetahs often live in small groups known as coalitions (discussed in the following chapter) and generally focus on larger prey to satisfy their collective needs. Hunting cooperatively allows them to take down large quarry such as near-adult wildebeests and zebras, targets beyond the reach of single cheetahs. Alternatively, they may make numerous small kills and I once watched two males kill three impala lambs and one young nyala in the same day, all of which were completely eaten.

Like males in groups, females are faced with increased energetic demands when they have cubs and cope by hunting more often and taking larger prey. The more successful a female is in raising her cubs, the greater the demands. For example, a female with five yearling cubs has to provide for the equivalent of slightly more than four adult females, an exhausting task. Cubs of this age eat almost as much as an adult, but are still poor hunters and very rarely contribute to catching prey. Mothers with large families often take risks, preying upon large species which they normally ignore when on their own. Such hunts may result in injury for females and I have seen them tumble violently when bringing down large prey such as male reedbucks. Luckily (and surprisingly, given the violence of some of the encounters), injuries incurred during hunts are usually superficial and cheetahs ordinarily recover.

It would make sense for cheetahs, particularly male coalitions or mothers providing for cubs, to scavenge meals but they almost never do. They occasionally steal kills from other cheetahs, but otherwise they generally eat only what they have killed themselves, even ignoring untouched carcasses of animals that have died of natural causes. Presumably, the possibility that some other, more dangerous, predator is lurking makes scavenging too hazardous. Cheetahs satisfy their daily requirements with often surprising versatility, but some behavior just isn't worth the risk.

# The Sometimes Social Cat

Of all the carnivore families, the cats are among the most solitary. Most of the 37 species of felids worldwide do not form the complex social groups that we see in other predators such as wolves, wild dogs and hyenas. The very conspicuous feline exception is, of course, the lion whose extended families may number more than 30. By and large though, cats are loners – but this does not mean they are entirely asocial. Males and females come together to mate and may associate for brief periods at kills or perhaps just for the sake of it. Recent observations from 'classically' solitary cats such as leopards and tigers indicate they probably spend more time with other members of their species than we thought. Additionally, for most of their adult life, females are accompanied by the cubs of successive litters, so while it is true that most cat species don't form the enduring, complex social bonds of a wolf pack or a hyena clan, they do not exist in a social vacuum.

In cheetahs, sociality is taken a step further and they represent a fascinating intermediate stage between the largely solitary lifestyle of most cats and the highly social lion. Female cheetahs are basically loners but males are sometimes loners and sometimes form long-term alliances with other males.

Let's deal with the females first. They follow the basic felid pattern. They are solitary and, except for the brief period when a female is sexually receptive to males, they have little contact with other adult cheetahs. Interestingly, unlike other cats, female cheetahs do not maintain a territory, the patch which an animal actively defends from intruders of the same sex. The general pattern among cats (at least the well-studied species) is that both sexes hold territories which they demarcate by various means such as urine, feces and vocalizing. This informs potential interlopers that the area is occupied and they risk an aggressive confrontation if the signals are ignored. Female lions, tigers, leopards and many other species defend their territories from unrelated females and occasionally even kill one another in clashes over turf. Female cheetahs, however, never actively defend an area from other cheetahs and therefore cannot be considered territorial. Rather than a territory, they occupy 'home ranges' which often overlap extensively with other females' home ranges. Female cheetahs largely ignore other females they see in the distance or actually go out of their way to avoid each other.

A female's home range may be huge. On the Serengeti plains, the average is around 310 sq miles (800 sq km) and may be greater than 465 sq miles (1200 sq km). Serengeti cheetahs follow the migratory movements of their main prey species, the Thomson's gazelle, and their home range size reflects the large distances moved by 'Thommies'. In areas where the game is resident all year round (in other words, where it doesn't migrate), female ranges can be much smaller. In some South African reserves, females have home ranges averaging around 40 sq miles (100 sq km). Because prey is fairly uniformly distributed at high densities, it means they do not have to become semi-nomadic over huge distances like females in the Serengeti. Although a small home range would be easily defended, South African females are just as non-confrontational as their Serengeti counterparts and do not adopt territorial behavior.

So, female cheetahs follow the felid pattern in being solitary but are unusual among cats in not establishing a territory. The social and ranging behavior of the males is equally atypical, though not for the same reasons. Unlike all other cat species (except for lions), male cheetahs form small groups called coalitions. When a litter of young adult cheetahs separates from the mother, typically they remain together for a while in a unit known as a 'sib-group'. The sib-group contains both males and females but by the time they are two years old, the females have gone their own way, leaving just the male siblings together. On occasion, males also seek a solitary life but ordinarily, if cheetah males have brothers, they stay together. Indeed, if a young male cheetah does not have any brothers, he may try to join up with other loners and about a third of all coalitions contain at least one unrelated member. Clearly there must be important advantages for males to have long-term companions rather than to adopt a solitary existence, but exactly what are they?

The key to the answer is, not surprisingly, territory. Unlike females, male cheetahs are territorial. Actually, it's probably more accurate to say they're territorial when they are able to be and being in a coalition seems to be a critical factor. Although single male cheetahs sometimes acquire a territory, coalitions have the competitive advantage in

*Coalitions of males like these three brothers will stay together for life. Unlike some other social carnivores like lions and spotted hyenas, even brief separations are extremely rare and group members call unceasingly for each other if accidentally split up.*

*Recently left by their mother, these two young males will continue to play*
*throughout adulthood but now have to devote more time to simply surviving.*
*Coalitions are usually pairs or trios but may number up to four.*

securing and defending turf. The edge becomes violently apparent in fights between male cheetahs. Territories are keenly contested and, as one would expect, singletons are no match for coalitions. Twice, I've seen pairs of males attack and kill single males intruding into their patch. One of these cases illustrates vividly the advantages of belonging to a coalition. At the time, I was monitoring numerous male coalitions, the most successful being a pair called Carl and Linford. Another pair, Rufus and Rastus, were in the process of establishing their own territory, occasionally making dangerous exploratory excursions into Carl and Linford's range. Inevitably, they soon met the occupants. Given that the encounter was fairly deep into Carl and Linford's territory, I expected them to attack, but amazingly, the two pairs sat about 200 ft (60 m) apart and merely watched one another. For about nine hours, they played a waiting game, neither pair apparently willing to make any sort of move. Carl and Linford eventually ended the stand-off by walking away, leaving the intruders to make

*Two brothers at play.*

their escape in the opposite direction without so much as a growl exchanged. Tragically, the apparently amicable arrangement was not to last. Only a week after this encounter, Rufus was killed in a poacher's snare, leaving Rastus without a companion. His wanderings took him back into Carl and Linford's territory, where, faced with only a single intruder, they were ruthless in defense of their land. In a fight that lasted only a few minutes, Carl and Linford killed the lone Rastus, mauling him savagely before finally suffocating him as they would an impala. The victorious pair incurred only minor injuries during the clash.

Compared with the huge home ranges of females, the territories of males can be very small. In a ten-year study made by Tim Caro and his team on the Serengeti plains, the average size of territories was slightly less than 15 sq miles (38 sq km) and was never greater than 29 sq miles (75 sq km). Non-resident males – usually loners who were unable to hold a territory – had very much larger ranges, wandering over huge areas in much the same way as females.

Of course, the reason animals defend a territory is for its resources and in the case of male cheetahs, the primary resource they're seeking is female cheetahs. Males attempt to establish territories in areas where females spend most of their time, thereby increasing their chances of meeting females and mating with them. In cat species where the female is also territorial, this is a relatively straightforward process; males attempt to acquire a patch encompassing as many female territories as possible. This is by no means an easy task and carries the very real risk of severe fights with other males, but the 'predictability' of female locations makes the productive areas fairly obvious.

Male cheetahs essentially follow the same process but it's complicated by the females being non-territorial. Their movements are unpredictable, so male cheetahs have to home in on areas which have all the characteristics that attract the roving females. In the Serengeti, females follow herds of Thomson's gazelles as they move between scattered patches of rich grazing. The key for males is to try to set up their territory in areas where the gazelles are most often found; where there are lots of gazelles much of the time, there will be lots of females. However, females also require cover, both for hunting and as lairs for their cubs, so the best territories are those which not only have many gazelles but also have numerous patches of bush.

There are very real benefits for male cheetahs in holding territories. Aside from increased access to females, resident males are usually in much better condition than non-residents. Also called floaters, non-residents are usually thinner, have more injuries, extensive hair loss, poor coat condition and ulcerated mouths, all symptoms of a much more stressful lifestyle. Floaters live a furtive existence in their effort to dodge resident males. They constantly keep watch, take brief rests rather than prolonged sleeps, move frequently at night and avoid prominent high points.

*Linford stands over the dead cheetah Rastus, before launching another attack.
For an hour after his death, the two victors remained extremely aggressive and
repeatedly mauled the carcass, as though making sure he was dead.*

It could be argued that the reason they are unable to hold a territory is that they are in poor condition in the first place. Indeed this may also be true and the two mechanisms are not mutually exclusive. Floaters may be caught in a no-win situation where their condition suffers because they don't have a territory, but they are unable to gain the benefits of a territory because their poor health puts them out of the running. Presumably,

*A male's scrape, indicating occupied territory.*

unless they are able to team up with another floater and challenge a resident coalition, they are doomed always to wander and suffer the apparent consequences.

There is one final interesting twist to the complex social mosaic of cheetahs. Although being territorial for males seems to be ideal, being a floater does not necessarily mean banishment to the fringes of cheetah society. Some coalitions never establish a territory and remain floaters, often intruding into occupied turf in search of females. For young males and males on their own, this behavior would be extremely dangerous and they tend to respect boundaries pretty strictly. But for experienced adult males, it might be just as beneficial a lifestyle, in terms of gaining access to females, as being territorial. As I saw when Carl and Linford met up with Rufus and Rastus, residents are cautious about attacking equally matched intruders. Coalitions of floaters might actually be able to locate as many or perhaps even more females by roaming around in search of them, rather than by defending a territory and waiting for females to move onto it. All of which illustrates that there are no hard and fast rules in cheetah society. No doubt as we continue to study them in a range of different habitats, we shall learn increasingly more about the factors which shape their intriguingly flexible society.

# The Next Generation

As discussed in the previous chapter, the unique social system of the cheetah is essentially driven by the need to acquire the resources necessary to pass on its genes. A female needs high densities of prey, not only for herself but also to be able to provide enough for her cubs. She also requires sufficient cover to provide safe hiding places for her cubs and for hunting. For males, their needs in the race to perpetuate their genes are simple – females (though they also need plenty of prey and cover for day-to-day survival).

The system obviously works; cheetahs find one another and females have cubs. But observing the process in action is extremely rare. Unlike lions, for example, wild cheetahs are very secretive about their reproductive lives. Males seem to find females opportunistically, either by encountering scent marks which they have left or simply by spotting females in the distance and racing over to investigate. In contrast to many cats, including lions, tigers and leopards, female cheetahs in heat rarely advertize their presence by long-range calls. Captive females sometimes utter distinct stutters and 'stutter-barks' when they approach estrus, but in such situations, male cheetahs are often nearby (usually in neighboring cages). The close presence of males probably stimulates the female to vocalize and we cannot assume that females in a natural setting use these calls to attract males from afar.

The female has other methods by which she lets males know that she is sexually available. Foremost among them is scent-marking. To carnivores (and indeed many animals), scent marks contain a great deal of information about the local community. Female cheetahs coming into estrus show elevated levels of reproductive hormones in their urine and feces which males can presumably detect. Males spend a great deal of time assessing such signposts and can judge their age. When they encounter a fresh mark deposited by a female ready to mate, they assiduously search the area for her, tracking the signals she has left in much the same way as a bloodhound follows a scent trail.

*The joys of motherhood. Cheetah mothers make very tolerant targets for their cubs' play behavior.*

When male and female cheetahs come together, it can be a surprisingly aggressive affair. Males harass and seem to attack females in spectacular displays involving a cacophony of squeals, growls and yelps as well as slapping and apparent biting. However, although they look stormy, the encounters rarely result in injury. Some observations from captivity suggest that the ritual is important in stimulating the female to be receptive to males and that the harassment may even stimulate her to ovulate. However, we have no strong evidence of this yet and the rarity of monitoring such interactions in the wild makes it difficult to confirm.

These 4-month-old cubs will soon be weaned.

What is clear is that the males stay with the female long enough to assess her readiness to mate. They may even 'guard' her for extended periods, presumably in the hope that she is approaching estrus. Most such associations last for just a few days but occasionally may persist for two to three weeks. Even a female with young cubs (and therefore with little interest in mating), is worth investigating from a male's point of view, apparently in the futile hope that she will ultimately come into season. I have seen males remain with mothers and their litters for as long as 18 days, regularly harassing the female and constantly smelling where she has been lying or any urine or feces she leaves.

Interestingly, during encounters where cubs are present, males largely seem to ignore the youngsters, even when they are not the fathers. This is unusual among the cat family (and many other carnivores) where males often kill unrelated cubs. Infanticide is disturbing to witness but males do it for a good reason. By killing the offspring of

*This 5-month-old is starting to lose the white mantle with which all cubs are born. One theory suggests the mantle mimics the warning coloration of the pugnacious honey badger, but considering cubs' vulnerability to predation, this is doubtful.*

*Two males (foreground and center left) rest with a female
(right) and her cubs. Groupings like this are temporary, only lasting until
the males are convinced the female is not ready to mate.*

another male (and here it is important to emphasize that they kill only unrelated cubs, never their own), the mother returns to estrus much sooner than if she were to raise the cubs. Competition for territories is so fierce that male carnivores often have only a relatively short period in which they can maintain dominance; if they were to wait for a female to raise the cubs fathered by a previous male, they might be ousted before she is ready to mate again and they will have missed their only chance to pass on their genes. The process is well known in lions where males that take over a pride usually kill all the young cubs sired by the previous pride males.

Why male cheetahs don't seem to engage in infanticide is a mystery but it may be to do with the non-territorial behavior of females. As we have seen earlier, female cheetahs roam over large areas and their movements are unpredictable. Whereas male lions which take over a territory know more or less where to find lionesses, there is no telling where a female cheetah might end up after males encounter her. If they were to kill her cubs, there's no guarantee that she would remain in the same area for any length of time and she might be just as likely to return to estrus in a neighboring male's territory or even a territory hundreds of miles away. Perhaps male cheetahs have little to gain from killing cubs and so they tolerate them. I should point out that we may yet see the behavior in cheetahs. While I have witnessed males tolerate unrelated cubs on a small number of occasions, we don't presently have enough observations to be absolutely sure infanticide does not occur under some circumstances. It may yet prove to be another fascinating component of the cheetah's unusual and often enigmatic social life.

When females are ready to mate, it will be the fortunate observer who witnesses it. Mating is very brief and, unlike lions, which copulate dozens of times a day, it occurs rarely. Breeding cheetahs only stay together for a few days during which mating episodes may be spaced by intervals as long as eight hours. It often occurs at night and cheetahs seek thick cover if there is any nearby, so actually observing mating in the wild is extremely rare. However, the gaps in our observations are no reflection of the cheetah's reproductive ability. Contrary to popular belief, they are prodigious breeders.

Litters may number as many as nine cubs, though more commonly range between four and six which, in any case, is more than most large felids. Furthermore, they have a rapid turnover in litters. Female cheetahs regularly conceive before their current litter has dispersed, which means they might be accompanied by large cubs while they already have another litter in the womb. Importantly, the female always leaves the first cubs to have the new litter, and youngsters may have only just reached their first year when the mother disappears to give birth again. In comparison, lionesses have a litter about every

*A cub watches her mother on the hunt.*

two years. Finally, if their cubs are killed, cheetahs are able to conceive again extremely quickly. Females have been seen with males the same day as losing cubs and have conceived as quickly as two days after losing a litter, though the average is usually around three weeks.

Like all cats, female cheetahs seek a secluded spot to give birth. Dens are usually hidden away in thickets of dense vegetation, rock outcrops (called kopjes) or in tall reeds or grass. Females move their cubs regularly, probably because the den site accumulates the cubs' smell after a few days and increases the danger of attracting predators. She carries them to new lairs, either in typical cat fashion by gripping them around the neck, or sometimes rather haphazardly by the body which is how wild dogs and wolves transport their pups. The cubs are born blind and helpless but open their eyes at about day ten and can walk by about the age of two to three weeks. At six weeks of age, cubs are very active and may already have been led to kills by the mother. The den is usually permanently abandoned before cubs reach eight weeks of age.

*Like all young carnivores, cubs are constantly investigating their world.*
*Even so, they are poor at spotting danger, a job which falls to the mother who*
*remains always alert for the appearance of predators.*

*At 9 weeks of age, this cub has left the den for the last time and will*
*follow his mother constantly. His best chance of survival comes from her vigilance and*
*knowledge of dangerous spots in the home range.*

From then on, they accompany their mother constantly, including when she hunts, although it will be many months before they can join in the chase. Young cubs sit and wait when the mother begins to stalk, and listen for her birdlike, chirping call once the outcome is decided.

Young cubs are extremely vulnerable to other predators. On the short-grass plains of east Africa, only one cheetah out of every 20 survives to adulthood. Most are killed by lions, though spotted hyenas and leopards also take cubs. There is even a record of a secretary bird killing a very young cub dropped by its mother in the open when startled by tourists. The period when cubs are still in the lair is the most dangerous. Karen Laurenson, studying females in the Serengeti, found that over two-thirds of cubs did not survive to emerge from the lair. Aside from predation, females are occasionally forced to abandon young litters if they have to cover large distances between the lair and the nearest food source – the reason productive home ranges are so important. Grass fires and exposure, particularly following heavy rains, also account for a small percentage of young litters.

Once they've emerged from the lair, cubs are less vulnerable because they can scatter and hide when attacked by a predator. However, the Serengeti's very open habitat offers few refuges and cubs are still at risk until they reach about five months of age when they can outpace most enemies. Fortunately, denser habitats such as woodlands may provide sanctuary for cubs. Suitable lairs are so abundant that predators rarely find young cubs. And thick vegetation also counts in their favor once the cubs have emerged. Where I have seen mother cheetahs encounter lions in South Africa's dense bushveld, the cheetah was able to distract the lions long enough for her cubs to flee and find refuge. Although lions are persistent in their search for cubs, I never saw them locate any and the mother was able to collect her litter once the danger had passed. Compared with the 95 per cent mortality rate of Serengeti cheetah cubs, only about 35 per cent of cubs die in the thicker bush of South Africa's dense woodlands where they have been intensively studied. Cheetah researchers are currently studying females which inhabit woodlands in the Serengeti ecosystem to

establish if they are more successful than mothers on the open plains. Although savannas are often portrayed as ideal cheetah habitat, the Serengeti cheetahs could not possibly endure if the 95 per cent mortality rate seen on the plains applied to the entire population. The woodlands are probably acting as a critical refuge for the species. We are rapidly realizing that habitats usually considered 'sub-optimal' for cheetahs are, in fact, crucial for their survival.

Given the many dangers facing young cheetahs, it's easy to assume mothers are doing a poor job and indeed, female cheetahs have a reputation of being shoddy parents. This probably arises from their helplessness when faced with attacking lions. In fact, cheetahs make alert, tolerant and often very brave mothers. Although they cannot possibly overpower a lion, mothers will charge much larger predators in the hope of momentarily intimidating or distracting them so the cubs can flee and hide. I once saw a female cheetah chase and slap a young male lion at least three times her weight before he seemed to realize she was no threat and turned to face her. By that time, her cubs had safely disappeared and she gathered them together once the lion had moved off.

Being a cub is a dangerous period but encounters with lions and other threats are actually fairly rare and most of their time is spent resting or at play. Games are extremely vigorous and athletic; despite their frail appearance, cubs are robust and spend hours wrestling, stalking and chasing one another. From the age of three months, cubs pursue each other and swat at their siblings' legs and flanks, the method used by adults to bring down prey. Such play almost certainly refines coordination and hones behavior which becomes crucial for survival later in life. I say 'almost certainly' because although play is widely considered to be an important rehearsal for hunting skills, this has never been tested and young cheetahs are quite poor hunters when they finally separate from the mother. Play behavior probably lays the foundations but we don't know exactly how important its role is.

More so than play, training by the mother cheetah is critical for the development of the cubs' predatory skills. Once cubs reach about five months of age, the mother cheetah begins catching small prey alive and releasing it unharmed in front of the cubs. Instinctively applying the same sorts of chase and tag tactics which form the basis of their games, the young cheetahs learn how to trip and subdue the prey. The cubs are exposed to important refinements which could mean the difference between life and death when they begin to take down more dangerous quarry. Once, I watched a mother cheetah release a fairly large impala lamb for her three 6-month-old cubs. They managed to take it down very quickly and one young female expertly grabbed the young antelope by the throat. However, she seemed unaware of the dangers inherent in the flailing legs of the distressed lamb and collected a hefty kick in the belly. Had the impala been an adult, the kick could easily have broken a rib or punctured her abdomen, injuries which might ultimately prove fatal. With her siblings still holding down the impala, the little female made a second attempt, this time approaching the prey from behind. She avoided the lamb's kicks and pulled its head backwards towards her, exposing the throat for the throttling bite which she held until the little impala was dead — exactly the technique employed by adults.

The earliest that cubs separate from the mother is when they are just over a year old and, in most cases, they will still be with her until they reach about 18 months of age. The actual separation seems to be a no-fuss affair; the only time I have witnessed it, the mother simply walked away from her sleeping adult-sized cubs and made no effort to re-join them. The cubs spent a few days calling for her but then seemed to realize they were on their own and began the task of fending for themselves. This can be a dangerous, difficult period for young cheetahs. I mentioned earlier how their hunting skills still don't match up to an adult's and they subsist mostly on small kills for a few months. However, their predatory skills undergo the greatest improvement during this period and by the age of three, they will be expert killers. Starvation is actually fairly rare among newly independent cheetahs, but they face a host of other dangers on the path to adulthood, many of which will dog them their entire lives.

*Whereas cubs are easily distracted, adults concentrate on crucial tasks like finding prey.*

# The Imperiled Speedster

In the early 1980s, felid geneticist Stephen O'Brien and his team stunned the conservation world with their discovery that cheetahs were as inbred as laboratory mice. Analyzing a number of genetic sites or loci had revealed that cheetahs showed the lowest variation of all the cat species. Even more compelling, when skin grafts were performed between unrelated cheetahs, many of the transplants 'took', a result normally restricted to very close relatives. The evidence suggested that some catastrophe had reduced the cheetah to a handful of individuals around 10,000 years ago. One theory even proposed that a single animal, a pregnant female, was the sole survivor of the crisis and that all cheetahs today are descended from her.

The 'cheetah Eve' hypothesis is probably a little far-fetched but the evidence for a population bottleneck, and resulting genetic similarity in the cheetah, is very real. And whether it was one cheetah or a dozen which saved the species, such uniformity is widely believed to have serious implications for survival. Low genetic variation is thought to hinder a species' ability to adapt to altered ecological conditions such as climatic change, the appearance of new viral and bacterial strains, or environmental changes wrought by man such as the clearing of habitat. The argument runs that if any single cheetah was vulnerable to one of these factors, then all cheetahs would be affected because, genetically, they are all so alike.

Even species with normal genetic variation may be profoundly affected by such changes. In the early 1990s, canine distemper disease jumped from domestic 'village' dogs into the Serengeti lion population, killing at least 1000 of the big cats. Many of those that survived probably did so because they had slight variations in their genetic complement which gave them some immunity, the same reason some of us suffer from a bad dose of the flu while a friend or work-mate might receive only a mild dose or none at all. Had the disease made its way into the Serengeti cheetahs, they might have lacked the necessary variation for even a few individuals to survive and the entire population could have perished.

Lowered genetic variation carries further consequences. Males have reduced sperm production and produce a high percentage of abnormal sperm, widely considered as one of the main reasons captive cheetahs are such poor reproducers. The sixteenth-century Indian emperor Akbar the Great kept some 9000 cheetahs during his lifetime, training them for hunting in much the same manner as falconers keep birds of prey. Although he tried everything in his power to breed his cheetahs, only one litter was ever born and it remained the only known litter produced in captivity until cubs were born at the Philadelphia Zoo in 1956. Extreme genetic similarity also predicts an increase in the number of cubs born with birth defects as well as more cubs failing to make it to adulthood.

But is genetic homogeneity really at the root of the cheetah's conservation problems? Almost two decades after the warnings of the geneticists, many of the dire scenarios they predicted have never been realized in the wild. For example, disease incidents are actually very infrequent in cheetah populations. While lion society provides fertile ground for disease transmission, cheetahs naturally live at low densities and interact with one another infrequently. As a result, an epidemic affecting an entire population of cheetahs is far less likely than it is for a richly social species like lions. Further, cheetahs can live in a surprising range of habitats and are able to tolerate some human activity, so perhaps they are not as sensitive to changes in environmental factors as one would expect.

Encouraging signs are also emerging to suggest that inbreeding is not compromising cheetah reproduction. We have already seen that they are excellent reproducers, capable of having a litter almost once a year with as many as nine cubs at a time. And, contrary to the expectations for a genetically impoverished species, congenital defects are very rare in wild births. In fact, only two cubs born during Karen Laurenson's intensive study of Serengeti cheetahs were affected by birth defects. Cheetahs do have extremely low cub survival in some habitats but, as discussed earlier, the main culprit is other carnivores, not birth defects or any other consequence of low genetic variation.

Research is also revealing that male fertility is not behind the difficulty in breeding captive cheetahs. Having long blamed inbreeding, zoos began discovering in the 1980s

A picture of health. Despite a close genetic similarity to the rest
of his species, this young adult cheetah will probably have little trouble
siring cubs – so long as he survives to hold a territory.

that changes in social conditions and other husbandry practices are the key to successful matings. Rather than housing pairs of cheetahs together (the traditional way to exhibit cats), keeping a female isolated from males until she comes into estrus and then introducing her to male pairs or groups greatly enhances breeding success, in essence, mimicking the process as it happens in the wild.

All of this suggests that if low genetic diversity is the cheetah's only problem, wild populations are overcoming it and it was never behind the reproductive puzzle of captive cheetahs in the first place. However, even if the genetic hazard is never realized, cheetahs are beleaguered by a medley of other, more immediate dangers.

*Radio-tracking and fencing off reserves are among the techniques contributing to cheetah conservation.*

Among them are the natural consequences of being such a specialized sprinter. With its lean build, small jaws and blunt claws, it is not a fighter and cannot afford to get injured in a conflict with other predators. Despite their bravery and bluff tactics, mother cheetahs are essentially helpless in the face of an attack on their cubs and although an adult cheetah can out-sprint anything on earth, it doesn't stand a chance against dominant carnivores if it is surprised.

On the open plains where cubs are so vulnerable, visibility and open space allow adult cheetahs to avoid attacks and few healthy adults die at the jaws of other hunters. However, in denser habitat, the balance swings the other way. While it holds advantages for females raising cubs (which are less susceptible because mothers are extremely vigilant), thick bush increases the risk of attack for adult cheetahs, probably because they don't see enemies approaching and also have more obstacles to impede their escape. I have seen lions or leopards catch and kill healthy adult cheetahs and one near-adult cub in dense bush on five occasions. None of the dead cheetahs were eaten; they were eliminated as competitors rather than killed for food. Population biologists have recently suggested that deaths of adults rather than very low cub survival is the main factor keeping cheetah populations small.

Lion-free regions remain the cheetahs' stronghold. Outside the national parks of east Africa, most predators are quickly killed by the pastoral Masai in defense of their stock. However, the Masai recognize that cheetahs rarely kill cattle, so human and big cat live in relative harmony. Furthermore, because of their reluctance to scavenge, cheetahs shun the poisoned bait laid out for stock-killing lions and hyenas. Freed of the harassment of dominant predators, cheetahs outside protected areas may actually be better off than those inside them. In Namibia's vast Etosha National Park, cheetah numbers are kept in the low hundreds due to pressure from competitors. However, on private rangelands bordering the park, lions and hyenas are heavily persecuted by farmers, who unintentionally clear the way for cheetahs to exist in a competition-free environment. An estimated 95 per cent of Namibia's 2000 to 3000 cheetahs exist outside protected areas on the rangelands. They are, however, far from being a perfect sanctuary.

People are still the most severe threat facing the cheetah today. Although the cheetah is tolerant of human activity, it needs large areas of natural habitat which retain high numbers of the indigenous antelope species. Where people clear such habitat for crops and replace antelope with cattle and sheep, cheetahs cannot persist. And even where habitat and prey remain, tolerance like the Masai's is rare; many farmers and stock farmers still shoot and trap cheetahs relentlessly. Although Namibia's cheetah numbers are the largest of any African country, they are only half the estimated population of 1975. During the 1980s, an estimated 10,000 cheetahs were killed or removed from that country alone, the great percentage lost on rangelands.

*This Zululand cheetah was killed by lions, intent on eliminating a competitor rather than for food. In more extreme habitats like the Kalahari, carnivores can't afford to be as choosy, and leopards and lions occasionally hunt cheetahs as prey.*

As human populations spread across the continent, conflict between people and cheetahs is inevitable and even where people are still scarce, the cheetah is rarely the winner. In Mali, Niger and Chad, Tuoareg and Toubou nomads assiduously hunt down the desert cheetah with saluki dogs. Cheetahs occasionally kill the nomads' young camels and goats, prompting tireless punitive expeditions until the cheetah, or indeed any cheetah, is found and killed. Even if a cheetah has committed no 'crime', the chance discovery of tracks is celebrated as another opportunity to hunt down the animal. So precarious is the existence of the cheetah in the extreme heat of the Sahara that it sometimes dies of heat-stress simply by being pursued. Cubs hidden by mothers in burrows are caught alive to sell as pets or, if they elude capture, are burned in the lair by stuffing it with blazing vegetation.

Even well-meaning people may unwittingly worsen the cheetah's plight. Despite the advances in captive breeding, capturing cheetahs for zoos may actually exacerbate their problems in the wild. Zoos have come a long way since Akbar the Great's efforts to breed cheetahs, but they are still the most difficult large cat to breed in captivity, a problem which some institutions overcome by drawing on wild populations. Approximately one-third of all cheetahs in zoos today were caught in the wild. With over 1200 cheetahs in captivity around the world, taking more cheetahs from the wild actually contributes to their conservation problems, rather than solving them. In a genetic sense, taking a cheetah from the wild is essentially equivalent to killing it; that cheetah will never make its unique genetic contribution to an already endangered wild population and most captive cheetahs will die without ever reproducing.

Although the cheetah may still be present in as many as 26 African countries, populations in only five or six of them are considered safe. A century ago, numbers were estimated at 100,000 and their distribution encompassed most of Africa, the Arabian Peninsula, Iran, Iraq, the southern provinces of the former USSR and the countries of southwestern Asia extending all the way to India. Today, the upper estimate of their numbers is 12,000, almost all of them in Africa, except for a tiny relict population of the once widespread Asiatic sub-species, now down to an estimated 100-200 individuals in Iran and possibly Afghanistan and Pakistan.

# Racing Against Extinction

The cheetah is caught in a conservation quandary. On the one hand, national parks and reserves, where human pressure is least, also protect lions, hyenas and other predators which keep cheetah numbers low. Conversely, outside protected areas, competing carnivores are few but cheetahs run the gauntlet of human hunters, farmers and other people who kill cheetahs on sight. Even without any intended malice to wildlife, humans alter the environment so radically that cheetahs cannot survive there. With such intense human and natural pressures, can the cheetah survive?

People are the greatest threat facing the cheetah today but also hold the key to its survival. And despite their respective shortcomings, both protected reserves and unprotected areas are critical for the cheetah's survival. Although cheetah numbers are never great where other predators are common, parks and reserves protect a core population relatively free of human persecution. So long as there are large protected areas, cheetahs will probably persist in them without any great effort from people. But of course, numbers will never be great and small populations are vulnerable to local catastrophes. So, even more crucial than protected areas are the communities that share their land with cheetahs. These areas have the potential to hold ten times the number of cats than reserves, but it is also here that the greatest challenge lies for cheetah conservationists. Unless an effort is made to foster understanding and tolerance for cheetahs among people who have competing needs, the species will only ever exist as small, isolated populations in parks. Fortunately, the process has begun.

Namibia is leading the way. Primarily led by conservation organizations such as the Cheetah Conservation Fund and Africat, farmer education programs are overcoming ignorance and teaching novel techniques which minimize sources of conflict. By corralling stock when vulnerable calves or lambs are present, cheetahs are less likely to be attracted to domestic herds. Another innovation, electrified fencing, is being used to exclude cheetahs from stock areas and farmers are learning that cheetahs usually ignore stock so long as their natural prey is present.

Farmers are becoming aware that outright extermination of cheetahs is not the most efficient way they can protect their herds and many ranchers embrace the chance to leave cheetahs alone, so long as the cheetahs leave them alone. The Cheetah Conservation Fund is even breeding and donating Anatolian shepherd dogs to farmers. Dogs are widely used in Africa to protect stock but traditionally used breeds herd the stock to safety when danger threatens. This creates movement and panic in the herd – irresistible to a sight hunter such as the cheetah. The Anatolian shepherd dogs are bonded to the herd and chase cheetahs rather than the livestock. With their reluctance to confront other predators, cheetahs invariably give way to the dogs and look for easier prey.

In neighboring South Africa, increasing wildlife tourism holds further promise for cheetahs. Landowners in marginal farmlands are realizing that the most productive use of their land may arise from the wild animals they had eliminated decades earlier. Farmers are gradually replacing their livestock with wildlife to attract the tourism dollar and big cats, including cheetahs, are high on the wish-list. Most of them come from places where cheetahs are in conflict with people. Despite the best efforts of the Cheetah Conservation Fund, Africat and other cheetah conservation groups, there is still widespread persecution. In areas where people simply refuse to tolerate cheetahs, capturing and translocating them to the emerging South African reserves gives a second chance to animals which would otherwise almost certainly be killed.

Reintroduction projects are not without considerable obstacles. Being captured and transported hundreds of miles must be a traumatic process and unless their distress is minimized, translocated cheetahs won't settle into their new home. Big cats have a well-developed 'homing instinct' and attempt to head straight back there, even if home is hundreds of miles away. This inevitably catapults them into conflict with people, the reason they were relocated in the first place, and few such nomads get another chance. Biologists overcome this by housing translocated cheetahs at the release site in large enclosures before they are set free, a process called a 'soft-release'. A few weeks of acclimatization eases the ordeal of capture and translocation, and within days of opening the pens, soft-released

Cheetah conservation at work. This cub (above)
was born to a reintroduced female saved from a
Namibian farmer's bullet. In turn, as an adult (left), he was
captured and translocated to become a founding
member of another new population.

cheetahs rapidly set about finding food and water, establishing home ranges and breeding.

'Reclaimed' conservation areas have many features to encourage success. A lack of resident cheetahs, low numbers of competing carnivores and an abundance of prey creates a 'cheetah-friendly' environment where the released cats quickly find a niche. In such ideal conditions, their numbers can blossom from a founding population of a dozen re-introduced adults to quadruple that in five years. Like a slowly forming jigsaw, a patchwork of reintroduced populations is gradually replenishing areas the cheetah once inhabited, as well as connecting isolated populations in established reserves. The South African projects are revealing critical information to ensure reintroduced cheetahs prosper, and that knowledge is being adopted by similar re-establishment efforts elsewhere in Africa, including Zambia and Zimbabwe. One day, the lessons learned from Africa may even be applied to countries where the cheetah is now extinct. I hope that in my lifetime, the cheetah will once again hunt the dry plains of India and the semi-deserts of Turkmenistan and Uzbekistan.

Zoos also have an important role to play. Many institutions now refuse to take newly caught wild cheetahs and are concentrating on improving the wavering reproductive success of the current captive population. Intricate and novel conservation techniques are being pioneered, including embryo implantation and artificial insemination. Indeed, some months before the ill-fated Rastus was killed by Carl and Linford, researchers collected his semen which, 18 months after his death, was used to inseminate a female cheetah in Rio Grande Zoo in New Mexico. The female, Sabie, had never reproduced naturally but following the procedure, she gave birth to three cubs. Two of them did not survive but the third cub thrived and is still alive today. She has been named Esperanza, Spanish for 'hope.'

All of which combine to give the cheetah a fair running start in its race to evade extinction. It certainly needs all the help it can get. Despite the dedication of cheetah conservationists and the species' own adaptability, the threats facing them today are greater than ever before. The cheetah's flexibility in different habitats, its considerable reproductive capacity and its ability to live alongside us is of little use unless humans decide to give it a chance. Like all large carnivores in Africa and indeed, around the world, the future of the cheetah is truly in our hands.

# Cheetah Distribution Map

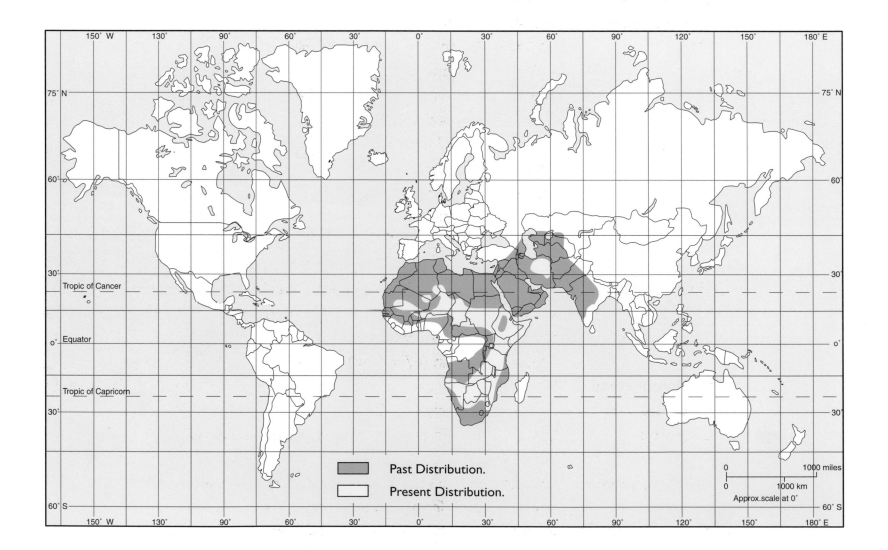

Past Distribution.

Present Distribution.

0                1000 miles
0                1000 km
Approx.scale at 0°

# Cheetah Facts

| | |
|---|---|
| **Scientific name:** | *Acinonyx jubatus* |
| **Common names:** | English: Cheetah |
| | Afrikaans: (South Africa, Namibia): Jagluiperd |
| | Zulu (South Africa): Ingulule |
| | Setswana (Botswana, South Africa): Lengau |
| | Shona (Zimbabwe): Ihlosi |
| | Kasanga (Zaire): Kisakasaka |
| | Fufulde (Cameroon): Siho |
| | KiSwahili (East Africa): Duma, Msongo |
| | Hindi (India): Cita ('spotted one') |
| **Weight:** | Males: 63–143 lb (29–65 kg) |
| | Females: 46–139 lb (21–63 kg) |
| **Total Length:** | Males: 68–88 in (172–224 cm) nose to tail. |
| | Females: 67–93 in (170–236 cm)* nose to tail. |
| **Shoulder height:** | Males: 29–37 in (74–94 cm) |
| | Females: 26–33 in (67–84 cm) |
| **Gestation period:** | 90–98 days. |
| **Litter size:** | Up to 9 but averages 3–5. |
| **Longevity:** | Up to 21 years in captivity, probably no more than 12 in the wild. |
| **Age at maturity:** | Females can conceive from 24 months and males are sexually mature from 12 months though usually don't get a chance to breed until their third year. |

* On average, females are smaller and lighter than males but sexual dimorphism is not as pronounced as in many other cat species, and size overlap between the two sexes is considerable.

# Recommended Reading

For such a well-studied and conspicuous cat, there are relatively few books devoted to the cheetah.

*Cheetah Under the Sun* (McGraw Hill, Johannesburg, 1975) by Nan Wrogemann and *The Cheetah: Biology, Ecology and Behavior of an Endangered Species* (Van Nostrand Reinhold, New York, 1974) by Randall Eaton are both very well-illustrated summaries of everything known about cheetahs until the mid 1970s.

*Swift and Enduring: Cheetahs and Wild Dogs of the Serengeti* (Elsevier-Dutton, New York, 1981) by George and Lory Frame is an absorbing account of one of the first detailed attempts to study cheetahs in the wild and includes many excellent firsthand observations.

*Cheetah* (Bodley Head, London, 1984) by Karl Amman is primarily a photographic account of the cheetah in Kenya's Masai Mara reserve.

*La vie sauvage au Sahara* [Wildlife in the Sahara], (Delachaux et Niestle, Paris, 1993, in French) by Alain Dragesco-Joffé contains a chapter on the Saharan cheetah with some extraordinary pictures of this very unusual desert form.

*Cheetahs of the Serengeti Plains: Group Living in an Asocial Species* (University of Chicago Press, Chicago, 1994) by Tim Caro, contains a wealth of information based on 10 years of observation of wild cheetahs in Tanzania. It is the most comprehensive account of cheetah ecology and behavior.

*Cheetah Survival on Namibian Farmlands* (Cheetah Conservation Fund, Windhoek, 1996) is a very good summary of the cheetah's conservation plight and an excellent insight into the work of the Cheetah Conservation Fund.

*Cheetahs as Game Ranch Animals* (edited by B.L. Penzhorn, S.A. Veterinary Association, Onderstepoort, South Africa, 1998) is a collection of scientific studies on the cheetah in southern Africa.

*The Natural History of the Wild Cats* by Andrew Kitchener (Cornell University Press, Ithaca, New York, 1991), *Great Cats: Majestic Creatures of the Wild* edited by John Seidensticker and Susan Lumpkin (Rodale Press, Emmaus, PA, 1991) and *Wild Cats: Status Survey and Conservation Action Plan* by Kristin Nowell and Peter Jackson (IUCN, Gland, Switzerland, 1996); these three excellent works on the cat family include sections on the cheetah.

# Useful Contacts

For more information or to contribute to cheetah conservation, the following organizations are worth contacting:

**Africat Foundation**
PO Box 793
Otjiwarongo, Namibia.
Tel: +264 651 304 563/564,
Fax: +264 651 304 565
Email:
africat@iwwn.com.na

**Cheetah Conservation Fund**
PO Box 1755,
Otjiwarongo, Namibia.
Tel: +264 658 11812
Fax: + 264 651 303 607
Email:
cheeta@iafrica.com.na

**IUCN Cat Specialist Group**
1172 Bougy, Switzerland
Tel/Fax: +41 21 808 6012
Email: pjackson@iprolink.ch

# Biographical Note

Australian born, Luke Hunter studied ecology at Monash University in Melbourne, gaining research experience with various animals ranging from gliding possums to marine turtles. He leapt at the opportunity to work at the world-renowned Mammal Research Institute at the University of Pretoria, South Africa, on efforts to reintroduce large cats into game reserves. He expanded his doctoral thesis, on ensuring the success of turning former farmlands into wildlife reserves, into post-doctoral studies at the University of Natal. Luke Hunter is now a full-time free-lance writer on wildlife and conservation issues.

# Index

*Entries in* **bold** *indicate pictures*

*Acinonyx pardinensis* 8
African wild dog 25, 29, 44, 69
Africat 63, 64, 71
Akbar the Great 54, 60
Caro, Tim 34, 69, 70
Cheetah Conservation Fund 63, 64,
  69, 70, 71
claws 13, 25, 57
coalitions 19, **24**, 26,
  30, **31**, 32, 33, 36
conservation 53, 54,
  57, 60, 63, 64, 65,
  66, 70
cubs **1**, **3**, **6**, 7, **9**, 10,
  **11**, **12**, 13, 26, **28**,
  29, 32, 34, **38**, 39,
  **40**, **41**, **42**, 43, **44**,
  **45**, **46**, 47, **49**, 50,
  **51**, 54, 55, 57, 58,
  60, **61**, **62**, **65**, 66,
  **72**
denning behavior 44,
  46, 47
disease 53, 54
Etosha National Park
  21, 58
farmers 63, 65
feeding behavior **17**, 18, 25, 26
fertility 40, 44, 54
fighting 33, 34, 57
FitzGibbon, Claire 17
floaters 29, 30, 34, 36
home ranges 29, 30, 34, 46, 47, 66
hunting methods 7, 8, 18, **20**, 21, **22**,
  **24**, 25, 26, 34, 39, 44, 49, 50, 57, 64
inbreeding 54
independence 22, 30, 32, 40, 45, 47,
  49, 50
infanticide 40, 43
injuries 10, 18, 25, 26, 34, 40, 50, 57
jaguar 7
jaguarundi 7

Kalahari desert 18, 59
king cheetah 8, 10
klepto-parasitism 25, 26
Kruger National Park 10
Laurenson, Karen 47, 54
leopard 7, 10, 18, 25, 29, 39, 47, 58,
  59

lion 7, 29, 49, 53, 54, 58
litter size 43, 54, 69
livestock 58, 63, 64
Masai 58, 70
mating 29, 34, 39, 40, 42, 43
mortality,
  in adults 29, 33, 34, **35**, 47,
    53, 57, 58, **59**, 60, 63
  in cubs 40, 43, 44, 47, 54, 58
O'Brien, Stephen 53
Pilanesberg National Park 18
play behavior 7, **32**, **33**, **38**, 39, 49
population bottleneck 53
predatory training 49, 50
prey selection 7, 17, 18, 19, 21, 22,
  26, 30, 64

prey species
  baboon 18
  bat-eared fox 18
  camel 60
  Cape fox 18
  duiker 22
  gazelle 17, 18, 21, 30, 34
    giraffe 18, **19**, 22
    guinea fowl 18
    hare 9, 22, 25
    impala 17, 26, 34,
      49, 50
    jackal 18
    Kori bustard 18
    nyala 18, 26
    ostrich 18
    reedbuck 26
    steenbok 7, 22
    wildebeest 19, 26
    zebra 18, 26
  puma 7, 8
reintroduction and
    translocation 64,
    **65**, 66
Sahara desert 21, 60,
    70
scavenging 26, 58
scent-marking 39
Serengeti plains 30, 34, 47, 53, 54, 70
sib-group 30
speed 7, 8, 10, 13, 14, 21, 22
spotted hyena 21, 31, 47
stride length 7, 10, 13
sub-species 8, 60
territory 29, 30, 33, 34, 36, 43, 55
tiger 7, 29, 39
van Dyk, Gus 18
vocalizing 29, 31, 39, 44, 50
vultures 25
zoos 54, 60, 66
  Philadelphia, 54
  Rio Grande, 66